Garfield

Here's Looking At You

JIM DAVIS

ЯR

RAVETTE BOOKS

First published by Ravette Books Limited 1985
Reprinted 1986, 1987
This edition first published 1988

_____

Printed and bound in Great Britain
for Ravette Books Limited,
3 Glenside Estate, Star Road, Partridge Green,
Horsham, Sussex RH13 8RA
by Cox & Wyman Ltd, Reading

ISBN 0 906710 74 X

© 1981 United Feature Syndicate, Inc.

9-1

© 1981 United Feature Syndicate, Inc.

© 1981 United Feature Syndicate, Inc.

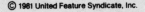

HEY, GARFIELD. LET'S SPEND TODAY CELEBRATING ALL THAT'S GOOD IN MANKIND

12-7

JIM DAVIS

LET'S DO A GOOD DEED FOR A STRANGER, STOP AND SMELL A FLOWER AND COMPLIMENT A FRIEND

THAT'S A HEAVY THING TO LAY ON A CAT FIRST THING IN THE MORNING

© 1981 United Feature Syndicate, Inc.

WOULD YOU LIKE TO GO CAMPING, GARFIELD?

JIM DAVIS

WHAT?! AND GET WET WHEN IT RAINS, FREEZE AT NIGHT AND GET THORNS IN MY PAWS?!

WE'LL HAVE PAN-BAKED LASAGNA

I'M PACKED. LET'S GO

5-18

5-19

© 1981 United Feature Syndicate, Inc.

GARFIELD! GET OUT OF THERE!

THE LIGHT **DOES** TURN OFF WHEN THE GLOVE COMPARTMENT IS CLOSED

JIM DAVIS 5-21

JIM DAVIS

5-28   © 1981 United Feature Syndicate, Inc.

5-29

1-14

ONE STEP CLOSER AND I'LL PUT THAT TONGUE IN A SPLINT

YOU GOTTA SPEAK THEIR LANGUAGE

© 1981 United Feature Syndicate, Inc.

9-3

© 1981 United Feature Syndicate, Inc.

© 1981 United Feature Syndicate, Inc.

YOU'RE NO LONGER A KITTEN, GARFIELD

9-17 JIM DAVIS

© 1981 United Feature Syndicate, Inc.

7-20

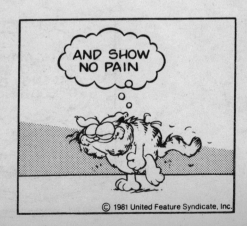

JIM DAVIS

3-6

© 1982 United Feature Syndicate, Inc.

© 1982 United Feature Syndicate, Inc.

AHCHOO!

© 1982 United Feature Syndicate, Inc.   3-10

© 1982 United Feature Syndicate, Inc.

© 1982 United Feature Syndicate, Inc.

9-17 © 1984 United Feature Syndicate, Inc.

DON'T TAKE THAT FLEA COLLAR OFF, GARFIELD!

WHO NEEDS IT?

© 1984 United Feature Syndicate, Inc.

11-15

JIM DAVIS

© 1984 United Feature Syndicate, Inc.

9-25

© 1984 United Feature Syndicate,Inc.

© 1984 United Feature Syndicate, Inc.

8-15

© 1984 United Feature Syndicate, Inc.

© 1984 United Feature Syndicate, Inc.

YOU AWAKE, JON?

OF COURSE NOT, DAD! IT'S 5 A.M.! WHAT ARE YOU DOING UP?

~CLICK

11-28 © 1984 United Feature Syndicate, Inc

I GOTTA MILK SOMETHING!

I'M LEAVING

© 1984 United Feature Syndicate, Inc.

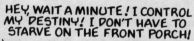

© 1984 United Feature Syndicate, Inc.

© 1984 United Feature Syndicate,Inc.

© 1984 United Feature Syndicate, Inc.

© 1984 United Feature Syndicate, Inc.

© 1984 United Feature Syndicate, Inc.

© 1984 United Feature Syndicate, Inc. JIM DAVIS

© 1984 United Feature Syndicate, Inc.

© 1984 United Feature Syndicate, Inc.

© 1984 United Feature Syndicate, Inc.

OTHER GARFIELD BOOKS IN THIS SERIES

LANDSCAPE SERIES

COLOUR TV SPECIALS

Here Comes Garfield	£2.95
Garfield On The Town	£2.95
Garfield In The Rough	£2.95
Garfield In Disguise	£2.95
Garfield In Paradise	£2.95
Garfield Goes To Hollywood	£2.95
A Garfield Christmas	£2.95

COLOUR TREASURIES

The Second Garfield Treasury	£5.95
The Third Garfield Treasury	£5.95
The Fourth Garfield Treasury	£5.95

Garfield A Weekend Away	£4.95

All these books are available at your local bookshop or newsagent, or can be ordered direct from the publisher. Just tick the titles you require and fill in the form below. Prices and availability subject to change without notice.

Ravette Books Limited, 3 Glenside Estate, Star Road, Partridge Green, Horsham, West Sussex RH13 8RA

Please send a cheque or postal order, and allow the following for postage and packing. UK: Pocket-books and TV Specials – 45p for one book plus 20p for the second book and 15p for each additional book. Landscape Series – 45p for one book plus 30p for each additional book. Treasuries and A Weekend Away – 85p for one book plus 60p for each additional book.

Name ....

Address ....

....